THE BEST OF
BRITISH COMEDY

PORRIDGE

THE BEST OF
BRITISH COMEDY

PORRIDGE

THE BEST SCENES, JOKES AND ONE-LINERS

Richard Webber

HarperCollins*Publishers*

HarperCollins*Publishers*
77–85 Fulham Palace Road,
Hammersmith, London W6 8JB

First published by HarperCollins*Publishers* 2008

1

A catalogue record for this book
is available from the British Library

ISBN-10 0-00-728529-9
ISBN-13 978-0-00-728529-7

'

Printed and bound in China by
Leo Paper Products Ltd

ACKNOWLEDGEMENTS

I would like to thank Dick Clement and Ian La Frenais for, once again, allowing me to use script extracts and giving up more time to be interviewed about *Porridge*. Thanks, also, to the actors I spoke to in the course of compiling this book, including Christopher Biggins, Sam Kelly, Tony Osoba, Philip Madoc, Paul McDowell, Philip Jackson, Paul Angelis and Peter Vaughan. Last, but by no means least, thank you to my agent, Jeffrey Simmons, Don Smith and my editor, Natalie Jerome, at HarperCollins.

EPISODE LIST

Pilot

'Prisoner and Escort' (transmitted 1/4/73)

Series One

1. 'New Faces, Old Hands' (5/9/74)
2. 'The Hustler' (12/9/74)
3. 'A Night In' (19/9/74)
4. 'A Day Out' (26/9/74)
5. 'Ways and Means' (3/10/74)
6. 'Men Without Women' (10/10/74)

Series Two

1. 'Just Desserts' (24/10/75)
2. 'Heartbreak Hotel' (31/10/75)

3. 'Disturbing the Peace' (7/11/75)
4. 'No Peace for the Wicked' (14/11/75)
5. 'Happy Release' (21/11/75)
6. 'The Harder They Fall' (28/11/75)

Christmas Special

'No Way Out' (24/12/75)

Christmas Special

'The Desperate Hours' (24/12/76)

Series Three

1. 'A Storm in a Tcacup' (18/2/77)
2. 'Poetic Justice' (25/2/77)
3. 'Rough Justice' (4/3/77)
4. 'Pardon Me' (11/3/77)
5. 'A Test of Character' (18/3/77)
6. 'Final Stretch' (25/3/77)

INTRODUCTION

You can count the number of *truly* classic British sitcoms on one hand – well, perhaps two. But however many hands you use, *Porridge* will be one of the first programmes to register for inclusion. Undoubtedly one of the real gems, the prison-based show starring the late Ronnie Barker as the recalcitrant yet loveable rascal, Fletcher, transcends the generations; like any other classic, it remains as accessible and funny today as it did when first aired in the 1970s.

Including the pilot, transmitted a year before the first series hit the screen, twenty-one instalments were made, attracting audiences of up to 20 million. Written by those prolific scribes Dick Clement and Ian La Frenais, and brought to life by an estimable bunch of actors, headed by the great Ronnie B as Fletch, a recidivist who spent most of his adult life behind bars, the sitcom quickly attracted plaudits and became a shining example of what good situation comedy is all about.

So, if you want to sample comedy writing at its best, find out how the series was conceived, discover some interesting facts concerning the programme and read about the writers' and performers' experiences, then put your feet up and keep turning the pages. Packed into this little volume are script extracts boasting some of the best moments from a superb comedy, an overview of the show's history and much, much more. Happy reading!

RICHARD WEBBER

THE STORY IN A NUTSHELL

'Norman Stanley Fletcher, you have pleaded guilty to the charges brought by this court and it is now my duty to pass sentence. You're an habitual criminal who accepts arrest as an occupational hazard and, presumably, accepts imprisonment in the same casual manner. We, therefore, feel constrained to commit you to the maximum term allowed for these offences: you will go to prison for five years.'

As the opening credits rolled at the start of twenty episodes of *Porridge*, these sobering words told us much about Fletch, everyone's favourite lag. From borstal to Brixton, he'd become something of a fixture in Her Majesty's establishments, having clocked up the years behind bars for an array of petty crimes.

His latest port of call was Slade Prison, a remote jail in northwest England, and we witnessed his arrival in the opening episode, 'New Faces, Old Hands', in September 1974. But it wasn't our first sighting of the forty-something lag serving time for robbery. No, we first met the cunning Cockney a year earlier, in April 1973, en route from Brixton to Slade in a sitcom pilot, entitled 'Prisoner and Escort'.

Writers Dick Clement (left) and Ian La Frenais forged one of TV's most successful writing partnerships.

The half-hour comedy was the second of seven pilots transmitted in a series titled, *Seven of One*; the BBC wanted a new comedy vehicle for Barker, just part of a package they'd used to secure the services of him and Ronnie Corbett from rivals London Weekend Television.

Clement and La Frenais, who'd already scored a small-screen hit with *The Likely Lads*, supplied two scripts: 'I'll Fly You For A Quid', concerning a family of gamblers, and 'Prisoner and Escort', which also introduced us to Mr Mackay and Mr Barrowclough, the prison officers tasked with escorting Fletch to his new home. Some people doubted a prison-based sitcom would have the legs to survive in the competitive TV world, but Barker wasn't one: after all, while planning an earlier set of pilots, titled *Six Dates with Barker*, he'd mulled over the idea of a prison series himself, so was delighted when the writers submitted their idea.

Initially, Clement and La Frenais envisaged setting their script in an open prison, while Barker felt a *Bilko*-style approach, oozing frivolity, was just the ticket. After much cogitating, they opted for a closed prison, affording the writers the chance not only to extract humour from the situation but to explore the darker side of doing porridge, too. There is no better example of this than the poignant episode, 'A Night In', the third instalment based entirely inside the cell occupied by Fletcher and Godber, the naïve first-time offender played beautifully by Richard Beckinsale. With Godber struggling to adjust to prison life, Fletch reveals altruistic tendencies to help his cellmate through his difficult time; in doing so, he develops into a father-figure for the youngster.

From the *Seven of One* series, Ronnie Barker enjoyed two major successes: as well as 'Prisoner and Escort', the Roy Clarke-scripted *Open All Hours* also originated from the pilot season. But while Clarke's offering relied more heavily on gags and comedy from the situation, Clement and La Frenais mined much of their humour from the characterisations, providing a depth which appealed to many.

Three of the four main players had already been recruited when the pilot's success saw a full-blown series green-lighted: as well as Barker, Brian Wilde and Fulton Mackay, who played prison wardens Mr Barrowclough and Mr Mackay respectively, also made their debuts in 'Prisoner and Escort'.

Jimmy Gilbert, executive producer on *Seven of One*, had known Mackay since studying together at drama school and working as actors at Glasgow's Citizens' Theatre in the 1950s. Hiring Wilde, meanwhile, to play the easily led and nervous Henry Barrowclough was Ronnie Barker's idea. In the pilot, it's Wilde – and not Mackay – who has the most air time with Barker, particularly when they hole themselves up for the night in a deserted cottage after the minibus transporting Fletcher

Porridge was written as a comedy vehicle for Ronnie Barker.

to Slade Prison breaks down on the bleak moors. But as the series progressed, Fulton Mackay's character came to the fore; on reflection, Dick Clement commented they'd under-used Mackay in the beginning but quickly involved him more. Identifying the tough-talking warder as a richer character meant Barrowclough's prominence diminished, much to the actor's disappointment.

A host of other wardens and prisoners were required to fill the fictitious Slade Prison, but the final piece of major casting involved finding someone to play Fletcher's cellmate – the

'Little victories, little victories.'

callow Lennie Godber. Ronnie Barker suggested Paul Henry, who'd make his name playing woolly-hatted Benny in *Crossroads*; having just worked with him, Barker deemed him ideal for the role.

Producer Sydney Lotterby had other ideas, however: he was impressed with Richard Beckinsale, who was playing Geoffrey in Granada's sitcom, *The Lovers*, and thought his sensitivity as an actor was apposite for Godber. When Barker saw the Nottingham-born actor in action, he shared Lotterby's enthusiasm. As soon as Barker and Beckinsale began working together, it was clear a dream partnership was forming.

For the sitcom's long-term success, it was crucial the principal actors worked well together; with most of the action taking place inside the confines of a prison cell, such a restricted environment would only magnify any deficiencies and incompatibilities between the principals. With *Porridge* this never happened, and the interplay between Barker and Beckinsale was one of the sitcom's many strengths.

With everything in place, *Porridge* made its small-screen debut with 'New Faces, Old Hands' transmitting on Thursday 5th September 1974, with just over 16 million tuning in. For a time, however, Clement and La Frenais experienced serious

Did you know?

While scenes set in cells or offices were shot in a BBC studio, the larger association area, where the prisoners congregated, was filmed at Ealing Studios, using a multilevel structure built inside an old tank.

doubts about how they could write a full-blown comedy concerning prison. They visited various prisons, including Brixton, and felt profoundly depressed because they realised there was nothing slightly humorous about the reality of life inside.

It was a chance meeting with Jonathan Marshall, who'd just penned a book titled *How to Survive in the Nick*, which provided them with the spark they needed. While having a drink in a Richmond pub, Marshall uttered the phrase 'little victories' which struck a chord with the writers, providing them with a valuable tool for Fletcher to exploit.

Over the next three years, a further 19 episodes, including two Christmas Specials, would be screened before Slade Prison finally closed its doors on Friday 25th March 1977, with 'Final Stretch' spotlighting Godber's release.

While the writers would have willingly written a fourth series, and the public would certainly have gobbled up more,

Did you know?

When the prison authorities refused permission for exterior shots to be filmed outside a real prison, numerous psychiatric hospitals around the London area were chosen instead.

it was Barker's desire to move on that brought the show to an end. However, it wasn't the last time we'd set eyes on the wily lag. A year later – Friday 24th February 1978, to be precise – we saw Fletch return to the outside world, his release

Messrs Mackay and Barrowclough's opposing styles created conflict at Slade Prison.

shown in the first of six episodes in a sequel, titled *Going Straight*.

After the final instalments of *Porridge* had been screened, writers Dick Clement and Ian La Frenais were invited to BBC Television Centre for lunch. During the meeting, the subject

Memories ...

'Dick and I thought "I'll Fly You For A Quid", the other pilot we wrote for *Seven of One*, would be the easiest to turn into a series but then Ronnie said it might be more challenging to make "Prisoner and Escort". The trouble was, we couldn't think how we'd sustain it – after all, how could you make life inside seem funny?

'When we wrote the pilot, concerning Fletcher being taken to prison, we had no intention of turning it into a series. So when asked to do so, it suddenly became daunting; we decided to visit various prisons and got thoroughly depressed because, let's face it, they are very depressing places. We talked to the governor of Brixton over tea at the RAC Club, visited Brixton and the Scrubs and ended up even more apprehensive. Then we spoke to Jonathan Marshall, an ex-con, about the routines of prison life – the meeting was valuable.

'We met for a drink in Richmond and talked about life inside. Suddenly, he came up with the expression, "It's all about little victories." He was referring to getting through one's sentence on a day-to-day basis, taking it a day at a time and earning "little victories" by scoring against the system. With that one little phrase we found Fletcher's character – it gave us a route in. That became the key to Fletcher.'

IAN LA FRENAIS

of Fletcher arose and Clement and La Frenais expressed an interest in following his progress in the big wide world upon his release from prison. Everyone loved the idea and before long the nation's favourite con – or, rather, ex-con – was entertaining sizeable audiences again.

Although an amusing series in its own right, *Going Straight* lacked the punch and richness of its predecessor. The confines of prison had created an edge which, frankly, was always going to be difficult to equal; furthermore, while Fletch was king of the castle inside, back on civvy street he was a loser, a man drifting along in life, struggling to come to terms with a world that had left him behind.

But the allure of *Porridge* remains, even now, three decades after the final episode was screened, explaining why it can rightly be classed as a *classic* of the genre.

'PRISONER AND ESCORT'

Fletch discusses his criminal background.

FLETCHER: When I left school I went round the local labour and appraised the professional opportunities open to me. Unfortunately my lack of scholastic achievement prevented me from doing the things I really fancied, such as stockbrokerin' or teaching tennis at a girls' school. And I didn't reckon working in a cardboard box factory. So I robbed the sub-post office off the North Circular.

BARROWCLOUGH: And you never looked back since, so to speak.

FLETCHER: No – nor have I ever been short of 3d. stamps.

BARROWCLOUGH: What have you gone down for this time?

FLETCHER: Aw, don't talk about it. Be a farce if it wasn't such a tragedy, Own fault, should have stuck to what I know best – housebreaking. But I lifts this lorry. Impulse steal. You know what I mean, impulse steal. I think it's a doddle, don't I?

BARROWCLOUGH: I gather it wasn't.

FLETCHER: Yeah, you know why, though – flaming brakes failed. Criminal letting lorries on the road in that condition. And he was overloaded. So there I was, with five ton on me back roarin' down bloody Archway.

BARROWCLOUGH: Wonder you weren't killed.

FLETCHER: I nearly was. Went through three back gardens, went clean through a brick wall and finished up in somebody's tool shed.

BARROWCLOUGH: Did they get you for wilful destruction of property? I mean, knocking that wall down.

FLETCHER: Yeah. And I asked for six other fences to be taken into consideration.

Memories ...

'I liked the pilot, it contained some wonderful material. It's only a three-hander but the contrast between Fletcher, Mackay and Barrowclough is very strong. There are two moments that are particularly funny: the first where Fletch pees into the gas tank – and I can still remember the laughter from the studio audience going on for a long time – and the second when Fletch escaped on the moors, runs around all night before breaking back into the hut he'd left in the first place.

'Ronnie's reaction, when he discovered where he was, was classic. I remember thinking what a genius he was then, because he was able to make that laugh go on and on. In hindsight, Fletcher wouldn't normally be the kind of person who'd try escaping because it would cause too many repercussions when he was caught. But you could argue it was an impulse decision: he suddenly saw an opportunity and took advantage of it. The main thing is, we thought it was funny and his reaction to it was better than anything anyone could have imagined on the page. Overall, the pilot was a great success.'

DICK CLEMENT

Barrowclough discusses his wife.

BARROWCLOUGH: Well, she sees a future of frustrated ambitions stretching before her. She doesn't like what I do or where we live. So over the years she's grown bitter and unsettled, full of restless urges, which have manifested themselves in various ways like bad temper, spots and sleeping with the postman. And there were liaisons with other men. We got to rowing all the time. Things went from bad to worse. Eventually we went to see the marriage guidance counsellor.

Did you know?

The gatehouse seen in the opening credits once marked the entrance to St Albans' Prison before, later, being acquired by the local council and becoming a depot for the highways department. Now, the building acts as headquarters for a mineral-water company's sales and marketing department.

Fletch took advantage of the weak-willed Barrowclough in 'Prisoner and Escort'.

FLETCHER: That help, did it?

BARROWCLOUGH: It helped her! She ran off with him.

FLETCHER: Oh well, you're well out of it, aren't you, mate. You're well out of a slag like that.

BARROWCLOUGH: She's come back.

FLETCHER: Oh I see … well, people change.

BARROWCLOUGH: I blame myself, I'm a failure. I'm only hanging on to this job by the skin of me teeth. I got so depressed I thought I'd take advantage of the prison psychiatric department. See them about my inferiority complex. Well, it's not a complex really – I am inferior.

Memories ...

'Barrowclough may have become a slightly one-note character, but he was a wonderful foil. When we spoke to people about prison life, there always seemed to be the hard bastard and the soft touch; there are comparisons in the army or the air force. Everybody knows the ones you can't mess with and those in whom you can see a weakness that can be exploited. Mackay and Barrowclough represented both sides.

'We deliberately set out to have a modernist and traditionalist; having Mackay as the old hard-liner and Barrowclough the new, relatively liberal screw created conflict and that's the life of our comedy.'

DICK CLEMENT

'I had lots to do in the pilot, whereas in other episodes I wasn't given so much. In the actual series, Barrowclough wasn't as important, which was sad. But we had a good company. You can't spend a lot of time with people without either falling out bitterly or getting on; fortunately we all got on well together.'

BRIAN WILDE

'NEW FACES, OLD HANDS'

Fletch and Godber discuss prison life.

GODBER: First time for me. Don't know how I'll get through.

FLETCHER: Cheer up. Could be worse. State this country's in, could be free. Out there with no work and a crumbling economy. Think how 'orrible that would be. Nothing to do but go to bed early and increase the population.

....

FLETCHER: My beloved Isobel. The little woman. Well, she ain't so little. I said to her the other day, 'Isobel, I'll never get over you, I'll have to get up and go round.'

Overleaf: Fletch became a father figure to first-time offender, Godber.

Memories ...

'In those days, before computers, we wrote in longhand on whatever was handy and then got it typed, correcting the text afterwards, if necessary. My handwriting is more legible than Ian's so it was always me who wrote everything down; when we moved onto computers it was still me, which was fine because I preferred it that way.

'One episode, "A Night In", was written one evening at the Midland Hotel, Manchester. We were in rehearsals with our play, *Billy*. Other times, we wrote around my kitchen table, surrounded by dogs and children, and with lots of interruptions. Sometimes I went to Ian's, other times he came to me. But wherever we were, it was always very chaotic.'

DICK CLEMENT

Memories ...

'Writing for Ronnie was the greatest fun we ever had, in terms of just the feedback. He possessed a writer's brain as well as an actor's and suggested the odd line or little ad-lib from time to time. He'd often do something and ask, "Is that alright?" After we'd stopped laughing, we'd reply, "Yes, Ronnie, fine." I don't think there was ever a moment when Ian and I looked at each other and said, "No, Ronnie, you can't do that." His instincts were spot on.

'He was also very respectful of our intention in the series and knew we weren't just writing a comedy. Originally, he saw it as *Bilko* in prison, but that's not what we wrote; he immediately realised that, appreciating that what we'd learnt about prison, about being a grim place, was reflected in the series – we didn't want to make it cosy.

'I remember early on, in "A Night In", giving Godber lines where he was wondering how he'd get through his sentence. It was an acknowledgement that prison wasn't a bowl of cherries and, therefore, a place to be survived any way you could, not just somewhere to make jokes about. We wanted to make it clear that it was a serious place and Ronnie totally acknowledged that and went with it, quite happy to play serious moments as well as funny moments. Therefore, it was a perfect collaboration in that respect; he tuned in to what our intention was – it was an incredibly happy experience.'

DICK CLEMENT

Memories ...

'Richard Beckinsale was an appalling reader but it was considered a coup getting him. If he'd had to read for the part he wouldn't have got it, but he was first to admit how bad he was. At the read-throughs, if he had a long speech the rest of the cast would groan and say, "Oh God!" He took this in good heart, though.

'I must admit, I don't know how he ever got his first job, he must have had a real tough time reading for it, from the page. With us, even by the time of the first rehearsal he was still bad: he was on the page but often read the lines slightly wrong – it was as if he'd just got out of bed. But by the time we did the show, he'd transformed his performance and was wonderful.'

IAN LA FRENAIS

FLETCHER: He brought me up from Brixton. Handcuffed we was. Well, you establish a rapport with a man what you're hand-cuffed to on a long trip.

GODBER: S'pose you must do. Specially when you go to the lavatory.

Richard Beckinsale turned in a fine performance as the naïve Lennie Godber.

'THE HUSTLER'

IVES: *(Shaking off sticky egg from his hand)* Oh Fletcher, not funny, not funny.

FLETCHER: Can't take a yolk some people.

Did you know?

Clement and La Frenais often turn to friends when naming characters. For Godber, they chose their London-based hairdresser and friend, Denny Godber, who – despite having sold his salon – still cuts the writers' hair whenever they're over from California.

Memories ...

'When I began playing Ives, I was also appearing as Rex in Eric Chappell's office comedy, *The Squirrels*. I'd do *Porridge* in the morning and *The Squirrels* in the afternoon. I played Ives for a few episodes in Series Two but became so busy I had to reluctantly give up *Porridge*. Each episode was beautifully constructed and the actual situation was fantastic.'

KEN JONES (Ives, a prisoner)

Ken Jones (right) had to give up the role of Ives when he became too busy appearing in office-based sitcom, *The Squirrels.*

'A NIGHT IN'

GODBER: This is the bit I can't stand.

FLETCHER: What?

GODBER: Lock-up. It's only quarter-to-eight. Barely dark. If I was at home now I'd just be going out for the evening.

FLETCHER: That's the point you see, son. We're here to be punished, ain't we? Deprived of all our creature comforts and the little things you've been taking for granted all these years like a comfy shirt, decent smoke and a night out.

GODBER: A night out …

FLETCHER: Look, if you're so keen we'll go out. We could find a couple of girls – two of them darlings what dance on *Top of the Pops*. Yes, Pan's People. Beautiful Babs – don't know what her name is. Arrange to meet them in some dimly lit Italian restaurant. Then we could go on somewhere if you like, some nightclub … dance till dawn. Then back to their luxury penthouse, and wallop. But you see I done all that last night so I'm a bit knackered. Also we'd have to get all ponced up and you'd have to darn me socks. So why don't we just have a quiet night in? All right?

GODBER: If you say so, Fletch.

FLETCHER: That's what you've got to tell yourself. You're just having a quiet night in.

GODBER: *(Gloomily)* Trouble is I've got six hundred and ninety-eight quiet nights in to go.

....

FLETCHER: Listen, Godber. No one asked you to eavesdrop on my dreams. It's about the only place you have any privacy inside – your head. You want to remember that, son. Dreams is your escape. No locked doors in dreams. No boundaries, no frontiers. Dreams is freedom.

Godber recalls meeting his fiancée.

GODBER: … that never-to-be-forgotten day when I met her at a supermarket in the Bull Ring – oh that's in Birmingham. She was stamping 'Special Offer' on giant-sized jars of pickled onions. I came round the corner from condiments and sauces and my wire trolley went over her foot. It was a magic moment. We both knew. I said to her straight off, 'Will you meet me outside?' I said. And she said 'All right.'

GODBER: When that door's locked I'm depressed and I'm afraid, and you – you know – just make it a bit more tolerable.

Did you know?

Amazingly, Ronnie Barker dreamt up the programme title, *Porridge*, the same time as writers Clement and La Frenais.

Memories ...

'I remember sitting with Ronnie in the canteen one day and he was tucking in to this enormous plateful of fried food. He looked at me and said: "I tell the wife I have a salad!" It was a lovely moment. Throughout the production there was such a nice feeling between Ronnie and Richard Beckinsale; it was like a father and son relationship. The atmosphere on the set was terrific and Syd Lotterby, the director, was wonderful and kept everything ticking along.

'I'd worked with Ronnie before on *The Two Ronnies* and *The Frost Report* and he respected other writers. Being a writer myself, I thought Dick and Ian's scripts were fantastic – and they still hold up in today's climate. They're faultless and not a line was wasted.

'Mr Collinson was a misery and one of those people who were fed up with life – a very sour man. But he was enjoyable to play.'

PAUL McDOWELL (Mr Collinson, a prison officer)

FLETCHER: You'll get used to it, Len. And the night's not so long, is it? It's your human spirit, see. They can't break that, those nurks. We'll be all right, you and me, son. Here, we'll go out tonight if you like.

'Cheer up, could be worse. State the country's in, we could be free.'

....

FLETCHER: I'll swing for you, Godber, I swear it.

The cell door opens.

PRISON OFFICER: What's going on here, then? Did you assault this man, Godber?

GODBER: He sat on my darning needle.

PRISON OFFICER: Is that true, Fletcher?

FLETCHER: Oh, naff off. Can't you see I'm in agony?

PRISON OFFICER: Why don't you get a move on?

FLETCHER: Why don't you go home and find out who's been sleeping with your old lady while you've been on night duty?

PRISON OFFICER: Oh, that's original, Fletcher, I've been having that for the last seven years.

FLETCHER: Yeah, and so has she.

'A DAY OUT'

Fletch, Godber and Navy Rum are heading off to help the local council dig drains. They're waiting for another prisoner, Dylan, before leaving Slade Prison.

DYLAN: Listen man, my name's Melvyn, what's all this Dylan scene?

FLETCHER: Not out of malice, son, we call you that out of affection. We calls you that 'cos you reminds us of Dylan.

DYLAN: Bob Dylan?

FLETCHER: No, that hippy rabbit on *The Magic Roundabout.*

The working party prepares to help the local council dig drains.

....

NAVY RUM: Hey, Ives, how did you work your way on this doddle? Bribed a lot of people in high places?

IVES: 'Ere, listen –

NAVY RUM: You're not a working man. Not a bird bones skiv-
ing little git like you.

Memories …

'This was a great joke, but whenever I watch myself in this episode, it looks like I didn't know what I was doing; I look very inexperienced. Mind you, it was one of my first TV roles. Syd Lotterby saw me in a *Play for Today* and obviously thought I was right for Dylan, the Huddersfield hippie, because it was the first time I was offered a job without having to audition.'

PHILIP JACKSON (Dylan, a prisoner)

'I think the series got better as we went along; the first was the weakest and contained some fillers. We were still nervous in this opening season, in terms of how do we get out of prison, how do we mix it up; but episodes like "A Day Out" turned out too broad so from that moment we decided to stay inside.'

IAN LA FRENAIS

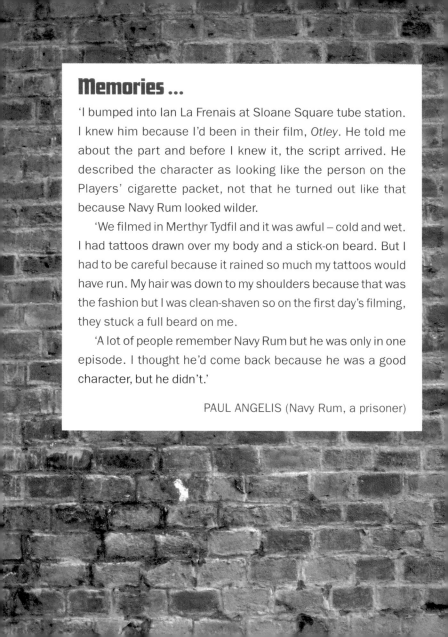

Memories ...

'I bumped into Ian La Frenais at Sloane Square tube station. I knew him because I'd been in their film, *Otley*. He told me about the part and before I knew it, the script arrived. He described the character as looking like the person on the Players' cigarette packet, not that he turned out like that because Navy Rum looked wilder.

'We filmed in Merthyr Tydfil and it was awful – cold and wet. I had tattoos drawn over my body and a stick-on beard. But I had to be careful because it rained so much my tattoos would have run. My hair was down to my shoulders because that was the fashion but I was clean-shaven so on the first day's filming, they stuck a full beard on me.

'A lot of people remember Navy Rum but he was only in one episode. I thought he'd come back because he was a good character, but he didn't.'

PAUL ANGELIS (Navy Rum, a prisoner)

'WAYS AND MEANS'

FLETCHER: All right, Mr Barrowclough, all right. We knows society's extracting its revenge on those what never had a chance to begin with. Look at McLaren here, never had a chance, have you, son?

McLAREN: Cowing used to it, ain't I?

BARROWCLOUGH: Yes, he's being punished just like you.

FLETCHER: Why? What did he do?

McLAREN: I spoilt the stinking soup.

FLETCHER: He spoilt the soup! And for that he has to pay the penance – well, what chance has any of us got?

BARROWCLOUGH: McLaren, that's not the whole truth as you well know. You spoilt the soup because you held a prison officer's head under it for two minutes.

McLAREN: Yeah, well …

BARROWCLOUGH: You tried to drown that prison officer, McLaren. It was a vicious and unprovoked attack.

FLETCHER: *(Amused)* Tried to drown him?

McLAREN: He cowing asked for it.

BARROWCLOUGH: You could have severely scalded him.

FLETCHER: Not in this nick you couldn't. Not with the lukewarm soup we get. Poisoned him possibly, yeah, could have poisoned him.

IVES: What sort of soup, was it?

McLAREN: Mixed vegetable.

FLETCHER: Mixed vegetable. Stone me, I bet he was furious. All those bits of barley and carrot up his nose.

Fletch is trying to get in the Governor's good books so arranges a stunt whereby McLaren climbs on the prison roof and Fletch acts the hero.

VENABLES (THE GOVERNOR): In the circumstances, I'm willing to listen to anybody. But what makes you think you can achieve what we can't, Fletcher? Do you know something we don't?

Memories ...

'This was my first episode and McLaren had a substantial part to play in it. Virtually everything about him was established in this episode. It was a fantastic opportunity and a great thing to do. He was hot-headed, aggressive, bitter and had a chip on his shoulder. It was the most important episode I did.

'Most of the long-shot exterior scenes were shot at a former mental institution, just outside Watford. As we filmed in the hospital there would be many people milling around the grounds: crew and technicians, cast, patients and hospital staff; it was difficult telling who was who at times. I remember standing talking to a female member of the crew and a hospital doctor. We chatted for several minutes and then the doctor suddenly pulled the woman's skirt up before running off. It turned out that "the doctor" was actually a patient!

'In this episode, the scene on the roof which ends with Fletcher sliding down the tiles and straddling a drainpipe always brings tears to people's eyes: tears of sympathy as well as laughter. That was filmed at an old school in London. It was fairly high but we were never in any peril because the pitched roof led down to a flat roof.

'McLaren had to be a tough character but humour had to come through as well and this episode is particularly funny. Making *Porridge* was a calm and civilised experience; it was such good fun and everything Syd did had a natural momentum. McLaren was undoubtedly one of my favourite and most important characters.'

TONY OSOBA (McLaren, a prisoner)

FLETCHER: I know something about what makes the lad tick. I'm not saying you're not an experienced man in these matters, Mr Venables – as is Mr Mackay, here, and Mr Gillespie and the Padre. But in his mind you all represent the establishment which only inflames his feelings of hostility and persecution. I mean the Padre's been out there rabbiting for two hours, and all he's had for his trouble's a brick up his megaphone.

VENABLES: *(To Mackay)* How is the Padre?

MACKAY: He's very upset, sir. Very upset that he couldn't get through to the man. Very upset also about losing two of his front teeth.

BARROWCLOUGH: There'll be no sermon on Sunday.

VENABLES: Thank heaven for small mercies.

McLaren (Tony Osoba) was one of Slade Prison's tough nuts.

'MEN WITHOUT WOMEN'

Fletch helps Warren and the others with a letter.

FLETCHER: Now, this letter of Warren's – it's very, very typical. It's your classic wives' letter after you've done eight months to a year – that sort of period. I mean wives make all those marital vows, but you have to be around to make sure they do love, honour and obey, don't you?

TOLLY: Yuh.

WARREN: Right.

HESLOP: Yes.

LUKEWARM: How true.

FLETCHER: You see, after a while a wife gets restless urges. So having got restless, chances are they weaken and gets naughty.

WARREN: I'll kill her. I'll throttle her.

FLETCHER: Yes ... that is one solution, but what we're looking for here is something a little more constructive. Besides, you're in here and she's in Bolton.

> ### Did you know?
> The theme tune was written by Max Harris, who wrote signature tunes for, among others, *Mind Your Language* and *Doomwatch*. The composition took two hours to write and three to record.

WARREN: It's visiting day next week.

FLETCHER: Yes, yes, we know. But if you was to strangle your wife on visiting day there's a good chance you'd lose half your remission.

WARREN: I'm just saying.

LUKEWARM: Ooh, he's so impulsive.

WARREN: I'm just saying.

TOLLY: Leave it off, Warren. Leave it to Fletch, he knows, doesn't he?

FLETCHER: Thank you, Tolly, for the vote of confidence. Now, where was I?

LUKEWARM: Just getting to the naughty bit.

FLETCHER: Oh yes. Now, having got naughty, she gets guilty. So in my reply that I've written out here I have sought to achieve subtlety with strength. An obvious display of affection but carrying beneath it a hint of menace.

Fletcher starts reading.

FLETCHER: 'My darling – I realise these are difficult times for you. Here we are, men without women – and you are women without men with all your attendant frustrations' – nice phrase that, isn't it?

LUKEWARM: Well chosen.

Memories ...

'In this, my first episode, I had to say, "Hello, Dad" several times which seemed to make Ian and Dick laugh, and thankfully they wrote me into more episodes where I had a great deal more to do. Ronnie was a delight to work with and I learnt a great deal from him. Always generous, he often made sure that the camera was on me for a particular moment during a scene together, very unusual in this business; and the way he could develop and add to an already very funny script was simply pure genius.'

PATRICIA BRAKE (Ingrid)

FLETCHER: Got it out of the *Reader's Digest*. 'I realise my love, that it is a lot to ask, to ask you to wait for me. But I will be upset, dearest one, if I hear about you having a nibble of something you shouldn't. In other words, dear heart, I have friends on the outside who have friends who have friends. And any word of hanky panky will be followed by swift and merciless retribution. I hope the weather is nice and you are feeling well in yourself. Yours etc.' blah, blah, blah.

LUKEWARM: Subtlety with strength, oh yes.

....

BARROWCLOUGH: I've never got used to bolting those doors. I think of you in that little cell … and I think of me going out of here, and going home, to my house. To my wife, who's waiting for me.

FLETCHER: What's wrong, Mr Barrowclough?

BARROWCLOUGH: I sometimes wish I was in here with you lot …

Memories …

'One of my fondest memories of this episode is when the wives were travelling to prison on a bus and one of them started reading aloud the contents of the letter. Suddenly, all the women realised that their letters were the same. One of the biggest laughs in a studio I've ever heard was when Lukewarm's boyfriend brought out the same letter – it was a moment of comic genius.

'I enjoyed playing Lukewarm; everyone in the cast was so nice. It's one of my favourite TV jobs and it's amazing that, thirty odd years on, it's still being played.'

CHRISTOPHER BIGGINS (Lukewarm, a prisoner)

'We thought we should have someone gay inside Slade Prison because it reflected the reality. I have heard recently that one or two people thought some of our remarks were not appropriate now, in a more politically sensitive era. But I dispute that because we wanted to cover the fact that there are gay people inside prisons, which is a fact. Fletcher's attitude to them was one of complete tolerance and to me that was more important – to show him being completely accepting and tolerant.'

DICK CLEMENT

LUKEWARM: Trevor's come all the way from Southport. He'll have had to close the shop. He's a watch repairer.

WARREN: I did a watch repairer's once.

FLETCHER: Yeah and now you're doing time for it. Did you get that, Mr Barrowclough?

'JUST DESSERTS'

Fletcher's pineapple chunks have been stolen.

FLETCHER: I don't know how to tell you this, gentlemen, but … there is a thief among us.

WARREN: There's nigh on six hundred people in this prison and I should think two-thirds of them are in for stealing something.

FLETCHER: That was stealing on the outside, Warren. Against civilians. That's work, that is. Making a living. Skullduggery. But the theft to which I'm referring has been perpetrated within these walls, which is despicable. A crime which offends the dignity of any normal law-abiding criminal.

An entire episode was dedicated to a stolen tin of pineapple chunks.

Memories ...

'We suddenly thought, "Wouldn't it be great to have a whole episode about something as microscopic as a tin of pineapple chunks." The idea of having one stolen item being used was quite appealing.

'Ian and I seldom had arguments about anything; we had disagreements at times where one of us didn't think a particular idea was working, or if we threw a line out and the other one made a face, then it didn't go in because we both had to agree it was good enough. But we seldom had a "slam-down" argument, certainly not on *Porridge*.

'The main debate would usually be trying to find the next plot. Sometimes they would elude you for a while, then you would get a handle on something which provided you with a way in.

'We'd ad-lib dialogue to each other – and still do; there's a sort of acting process to it in a strange way. Occasionally you'll throw a line at somebody or respond in the other character's voice, just to see what happens.'

DICK CLEMENT

Lukewarm (Christopher Biggins, left) had a cosy job in the kitchen.

'HEARTBREAK HOTEL'

Fletcher turns off the radio.

GODBER: Here, I was listening to that.

'Barrowclough's a vitamin freak. He takes so many tablets, I should think when he makes love he rattles.'

FLETCHER: Yeah, well, I'm not. Teenage sentimental slush.

GODBER: I have to sit through your *Gardeners' Question Time* and *Friday Night is Music Night*.

FLETCHER: All right, all right. And I sit through *Rosko's Round Table* but I draw the line at David 'Diddy' Hamilton. The wireless is never off in this nick.

GODBER: Well, the screws think it makes us work harder. They're piping Tony Blackburn through to the kitchens now.

FLETCHER: They're doing that 'cos they believe we're in prison to be punished.

....

On Godber's behalf, Fletch asks Mackay about radio requests.

FLETCHER: Miss Lonely Loins here, lovelorn Lennie, he wants to know whether the BBC plays prisoners' requests.

MACKAY: No. The answer to that is no, on the grounds that it causes embarrassment.

GODBER: Embarrassment?

MACKAY: To the prisoners' families. The family might have excused his absence by telling the neighbours that the felon in question was abroad, or working on a North Sea oil rig.

Memories ...

'Fulton put in a brilliant performance as Mr Mackay. He'd come from years of serious, straight Scottish theatre, yet took to comedy like a duck to water. But he was very pernickety: I remember one day sitting in the producer's box with Syd Lotterby, who shouted: "Oh, come on, Fulton, for god's sake!" Fulton couldn't hear him, of course. I suspect that sort of thing went on more often than we knew. But although Fulton was very particular, the end result was extremely good.'

SAM KELLY (Warren, a prisoner)

GODBER: Oh I see.

MACKAY: No doubt your wife, Fletcher, has told your friends that you're on a five-year safari.

FLETCHER: No, no. She tells them I'm doing missionary work in Scotland.

MACKAY: No, Godber. The practice was also open to abuse. There was nothing to stop prisoners sending messages in code across our airways.

FLETCHER: Ah, that's a point – yeah, that's a point. Listen to some heart-warming Christmas message from some poor lag. To his beloved wife and family and little Tiny Tim. Could he please hear Harry Secombe with *The Impossible Dream*. Translated what he really meant was 'Nobby, have the ladder round the back of E Wing, Boxing Day – and bring me a mince pie.'

Mr Mackay was a strict disciplinarian and feared by many of Slade Prison's inmates.

MACKAY: Six rolls of soft toilet paper have disappeared from the Governor's closet – the Governor's own personal water closet.

FLETCHER: Oh dear. Would you Adam and Eve it? What next?

MACKAY: Knowing you, Fletcher, probably the seat.

FLETCHER: Don't look at me.

GODBER: Nor me, it's writing paper I'm short of …

MACKAY: It's not right. We've had to give the Governor standard prison issue tissue.

GODBER: That's rough.

FLETCHER: Not half, it ain't. That'll wipe the smile off his face.

It's visiting time and Godber sees Ingrid, Fletch's daughter and his soon-to-be new fiancée, for the first time.

INGRID: Hello, Dad.

FLETCHER: Hello, Ingrid, love.

GODBER: Hello, Mum.

MRS GODBER: Hello, son.

Godber only had eyes for Fletch's daughter, Ingrid, when she visited the prison.

Fletcher registers Godber's visitor and Godber makes the introductions.

GODBER: Oh, er – this is me mum, Fletch.

MRS GODBER: Hello, Mr Fletcher.

FLETCHER: Oh, pleasure's mine, Mrs Godber. Got a fine lad there. This is my eldest, Ingrid.

INGRID: Hello.

MACKAY: Sit down, Fletcher! And you, Godber! This is not a royal garden party.

INGRID: Who's he, then?

FLETCHER: That's Mr Mackay, Charmless Celtic, nurk.

INGRID: And who's the boy?

FLETCHER: Oh, that's Lennie. Lennie Godber, my temporary cellmate. He's from Birmingham but he's got an O-level in geography.

Memories ...

'Introducing Ingrid, as Fletcher's daughter, worked well because it was nice having a woman in the show, from time to time. The character was very funny and it paid off later on because Godber fancied her, which gave us dialogue in the cell as well; it also enabled us to provide some background and substance to Fletch. Ingrid was very useful, particularly in the early series. I don't think I knew Patricia Brake, who played her, although I'd probably seen her in a couple of television pieces; but we were pleased with how she got on; to be honest, I don't think there was any casting we weren't pleased with.'

DICK CLEMENT

INGRID: Oh.

FLETCHER: Well, you have to find your way round Birmingham.

....

Fletcher asks Ingrid about his son, Raymond.

FLETCHER: And how's young Raymond?

INGRID: Oh, Raymond won the mile in the school sports.

FLETCHER: Oh, did he? Wish I had, I might not be in here now.

....

FLETCHER: I'm talking about standards, moral standards. All these social commentators, they don't know Britain. They all live within a stone's throw of each other in NW1. They ain't never been north of Hampstead or south of Sloane Square. But in the real world – Birmingham, Bristol, Muswell Hill – the fundamentals haven't changed – here, are you wearing a bra?

INGRID: I don't need to, Dad.

FLETCHER: You what?

Memories ...

'In this episode, I appeared not wearing a bra, very risqué in 1975; hanging on my bathroom wall now is a certificate made by the props department commemorating this momentous occasion. I'm so proud to have been part of *Porridge* and watch the repeats with delight.'

PATRICIA BRAKE (Ingrid)

INGRID: I haven't done for years. My breasts are firm and pliant.

FLETCHER: Ingrid, please, This ain't San Tropay you know, this is Slade bleedin' Prison. There's six hundred men in here who'd go berserk at a glimpse of skin, never mind unfettered knockers.

....

Godber has fallen for Ingrid.

GODBER: Oh, Fletch – can I ask you something?

FLETCHER: Feel free.

GODBER: You know when I was very down the other day. After Denise's letter.

FLETCHER: Yes.

GODBER: When I was worried about the stigma of being an ex-con …

FLETCHER: Yes …

GODBER: Well, will it be a problem for me? I mean, will I be able to work me way back into society?

FLETCHER: That depends, son. Depends on the breaks.

GODBER: Have there been any problems for you? When you get out?

Did you know?

Real-life prison officers have admitted that the humour of *Porridge* is very realistic. One, when starting his job, was even informed that during his career he'd meet every one of the characters seen in the sitcom.

FLETCHER: Not for me, no. I've never had to worry about no references, no testimonials. 'Cos I've always gone straight, straight back into crime. It's different with you, Lennie – you're young, you're healthy, you've got an honest face.

GODBER: Is that enough?

FLETCHER: Yes, yes. Character. That's what I can read. And you've got it, son. You're a good lad.

GODBER: So, you think, if someone really cared for me, a girl, like … she'd overlook my past misdemeanours?

> ### Did you know?
> Fulton Mackay was passionate about art and a keen painter. Also a writer, he completed several romantic plays about Scotland.

FLETCHER: Certainly, if she's any sort of human being of course she would. Like anybody would, Lennie, my son, you have to learn to believe in yourself. I believe in you.

GODBER: Do you, Fletch?

FLETCHER: 'Course I do.

GODBER: Oh good, I'm going to send this, then. *(He holds up a letter.)* Would you give it to your mucker, Barrowclough – to post in the village?

FLETCHER: *(Reading the address)* BBC …?

GODBER: It's on plain notepaper, so they won't know it's from a prisoner.

FLETCHER: 'Hello, Young Lovers Corner'. Oh gawd. Is all this soul-searching for the benefit of that slag Denise?

GODBER: No, not her.

FLETCHER: Well who?

GODBER: Ingrid.

Did you know?

Richard Beckinsale won an award as Best TV Newcomer in 1971 after appearing as Geoffrey in the Granada sitcom, *The Lovers*.

FLETCHER: My Ingrid …

GODBER: *(Quoting his letter)* Yeah … 'Our eyes met across a crowded room …'

FLETCHER: My daughter, Ingrid?

GODBER: 'And though we didn't know each other, we both knew …'

FLETCHER: *(Exploding)* You think I'd let my beloved Ingrid take up with the likes of you! A bleeding juvenile delinquent from the backstreets of Birmingham!

He raises his fist, about to bring it down on Godber.

'DISTURBING THE PEACE'

Fletch tells Barrowclough that he plans to write a book.

BARROWCLOUGH: Book!

FLETCHER: Well, working in the library has rekindled my literary aspirations. So I'm working on this book, see. On prison life. From the man within, like.

BARROWCLOUGH: *(Not keen)* Prison life.

Overleaf: Fletch could twist Mr Barrowclough (Brian Wilde) around his little finger.

FLETCHER: Ah, but don't worry, I'm very objective. I haven't overlooked the difficult task which confronts you brave boys in blue and I've sought to shed light on your problems as much as the ones faced by my fellow felons.

BARROWCLOUGH: *(Reassured)* Oh good, good. What are you going to call your book, Fletcher?

FLETCHER: *Don't Let the Bastards Grind You Down*.

....

With Mackay on a course, the tough-talking Mr Wainwright is drafted in to replace him. Eager to get rid of him, the prisoners stage a mock riot in the canteen.

McLAREN: Hey you, I'm talking to you.

GODBER: Me?

McLAREN: Yes you, Fanny Craddock … there's a caterpillar on my plate.

GODBER: Well a caterpillar don't eat much.

McLAREN: You what?

Memories ...

'This episode was enormous fun with Peter Jeffrey playing Mr Wainwright, a warden who replaces Mr Mackay while he attends a course. In one scene, there was a riot in the canteen with food being thrown everywhere. Because we didn't complete the filming at the end of the session, we had to return the following day.

'Due to continuity, we had to wear the same costume, even though it was stained and had congealed food all over it from the great food fight in the canteen previously; when you moved your arm the uniform almost cracked! The floor was also still slippery with all the muck that had been thrown around and the smell was awful.

'But the episode itself was hysterically funny with Barrowclough made to look as if he was the only man in the prison who can quell this appalling riot and send Wainwright packing with his tail between his legs. It was huge fun and one of my favourites.'

TONY OSOBA (McLaren, a prisoner)

Philip Madoc (left) made his only appearance as oddball Williams.

GODBER: Ease up, Mac, it's only a make-believe riot.

McLAREN: I know, kid, but I have to make it look authentic.

....

With Mackay away for a few days, Fletch suggests to fellow inmates that they organise some gambling, suggesting frog racing.

WILLIAMS: Should I tell you something about frogs? Which is a fact. Like me, the frog has an exceptional sexual appetite. When the frog and his mate, mate, he's at it for twenty-eight days non-stop.

GODBER: Twenty-eight days!

WILLIAMS: Non-stop.

FLETCHER: No wonder his eyes bulge out.

Memories ...

'Ronnie phoned me, even though I didn't really know him then. He told me there was a part coming up and he wanted me to play it. He was the best actor of comedy around and I didn't think twice about doing it.

'When it came to recording the main joke, about frogs, I could only get out about half a dozen words before the audience began laughing. Richard [Beckinsale] was sitting beside me, just watching. Because the studio audience were laughing so much, he was just waiting for me to corpse.

'It was a perfectly constructed scene. Williams was a bit of an oddball and I heard later that they would have like to have put him in as a permanent character but Dick Clement and Ian La Frenais were in America and by the time they were able to get hold of them, they'd already planned the next series.'

PHILIP MADOC (Williams, a prisoner)

'NO PEACE FOR THE WICKED'

Fletcher's description of Ives when Banyard is discussing acting.

BANYARD: You don't necessarily have to act. You could be prompter or work the lights or operate the wind machine.

FLETCHER: The wind machine, what you want one of those for? Just enlist Ives, he's a walking wind machine he is.

Blanco, who's at a loose end, visits Fletch.

BLANCO: D'you know … I'm at a bit of a loose end.

FLETCHER: Yes, well I expect you are, Blanco. You could always study – improve your mind.

BLANCO: I tried that once: I got a book out of the library, on memory training. Studied it for months. Then I had to pack it in.

FLETCHER: Why?

BLANCO: I forgot where I left the book.

Did you know?

When the third series was being recorded, Clement and La Frenais were in the States and would carry out rewrites over the phone. Fortunately, the scripts rarely changed.

David Jason spent hours in the make-up room being transformed into Blanco, Slade Prison's aged inmate.

Memories ...

'Ives was definitely a sneaky little bastard who you always had to watch out for. In fact, we had a couple of others who were very similar, like Harris, who was played by Ronald Lacey. Obviously, you'll get nasty characters in prison and that's what we had to show.'

DICK CLEMENT

'David Jason was playing an old man when, in fact, he was much younger, but he'd done that quite a lot. Ronnie knew him well, liked him and felt comfortable with him. That was important and is part of the overall process of making a successful show.'

DICK CLEMENT

Visitors chat to Fletcher in his cell. Mackay feels it's time to move on.

MACKAY: Perhaps you would like to see the recreation room?

OLDER MAN: Yes, we're rather disturbing this man's privacy.

FLETCHER: Privacy! Precious little of that in here.

MACKAY: Fletcher!

YOUNGER MAN: No, no, please, let the man speak.

FLETCHER: Well, have you noticed any signs of privacy on your rounds? Seen a door without a peephole? Seen a shower curtain or a cubicle door in the latrines? Very hard, you know, to retain a vestige of human dignity when you're sitting on the bog and a whole football team clatters past on their way to the showers.

'HAPPY RELEASE'

Fletcher, who's in the hospital ward, talks to Godber.

FLETCHER: Can't complain. Life of Riley, ain't it? And I had a nice day out, Lennie. Went down to Carlisle General and got plastered. And there was some lovely nurses there – kept popping their heads round the door, giggling like. 'Cos there I was, a convict. Mister Menace – handcuffed to a wheelchair.

GODBER: Sort of like Ironside – only bent.

....

Blanco taking a long time to explain something.

FLETCHER: Will this take long, Blanco – only my foot's gone to sleep, and I'd like to catch it up.

Fletcher thinking he's been molested.

FLETCHER: I was awoken, Mr Barrowclough. Woken by a foreign hand.

BARROWCLOUGH: A foreign hand?

FLETCHER: Well, you know what I mean, Norris was over here, sir.

BARROWCLOUGH: *(Looking at Norris)* What were you up to – stealing?

NORRIS: I haven't been up to anything.

FLETCHER: Don't give me that, you were over here rummaging in my pyjamas.

BARROWCLOUGH: Have you got any valuables here, Fletcher?

FLETCHER: Only what I always keep in my pyjamas.

BLANCO: He could have been after your lemon barley water.

FLETCHER: What – in my pyjamas? Funny shaped bottle.

BARROWCLOUGH: What have you got to say for yourself, Norris?

NORRIS: What's he got that I'd want to nick? One orange and a pair of smelly slippers.

'THE HARDER THEY FALL'

Godber is learning Spanish.

FLETCHER: Gawd, Godber, you've been taking every miffing course in this prison – arts and crafts, O-levels, pottery, Spanish. What are you going to do with Spanish, become an interpreter, are you?

GODBER: Si, si, Señor.

FLETCHER: That's it, is it? Six weeks of concentrated study and what have we got – 'Si, si, Señor'!

GODBER: No, listen … No tiene vaca, pero tiene uno burro.

FLETCHER: Go on then, I'll buy it.

GODBER: I haven't got a cow, but I have got a donkey.

FLETCHER: Oh that'll come in handy – that's extremely useful, that is. On your first Spanish holiday, pick up a shy little señorita, she starts whispering sweet nothings up your nose and what do you say? 'Well, I haven't got a cow, darling, but I have got a donkey.'

....

FLETCHER: I don't reckon boxing's such a noble art at all.

MACKAY: No?

FLETCHER: I had a friend once – haven't told you this before, have I? He was a light-heavy. Good, strong boy. Won a few fights. Suddenly thought he was the bee's knees – fast cars, easy women. Classic story of too much, too soon. He just blew up. He got into debt and ended up in one of those travelling booths. Four fights a night, seven nights a week. Well the body can't take that punishment. His brain went soft, his reflexes went. You know – punchy. Just became like a vegetable, an incoherent non-thinking zombie.

MACKAY: What became of him?

FLETCHER: He joined the prison service as a warder. Doing very well.

....

We see Grouty's cell. It's an extremely well-furnished single cell with a quilted counterpane on the bed, an expensive radio and record player, a lamp made from an old Chianti bottle and several framed pictures of friends and well-known sporting personalities. He also has chintzy curtains, a rug, magazine rack and a budgie in a cage. Harry Grout himself is a heavy-set man; an affable East London villain though one should be aware of a sense of power when he chooses to switch off the charm. He is listening to the radio on stereo headphones when Fletcher enters. Harry looks up and sees him, indicating that he should wait a moment till he has finished listening. Fletcher enters the cell, looks around, touches the birdcage and waits.

GROUTY: *Archers*. Never miss.

FLETCHER: They still on, are they?

GROUTY: Doris is in a bit of a state. She's got Dutch Elm disease.

FLETCHER: Oh dear, poor Doris.

GROUTY: Don't you follow *The Archers?*

FLETCHER: I don't Grouty. Not for some years. Not since Grace copped it when I was in Shepton Mallet. That's nice.

Grout is putting on a dressing gown.

FLETCHER: I like the radio, mind. *Gardeners' Question Time* and *Desert Island Discs*.

GROUTY: I like a good play myself. And a *Book at Bedtime,* never miss that.

FLETCHER: I like that. But of course they don't allow us the wireless that late.

GROUTY: Don't they? No one's ever told me.

FLETCHER: Don't suppose anyone's every dared. Nice place you got here.

GROUTY: Do you like it?

FLETCHER: All the creature comforts. Like the lamp.

GROUTY: Memento. Of Alassio. That's in Italy that is.

FLETCHER: Wasn't it Alassio that they extradited you from?

Grouty (Peter Vaughan) was the godfather of Slade Prison.

Memories ...

'I enjoyed the role immensely, it was a brilliant piece of writing. Although he didn't do a great number of episodes, he was very prominent in the minds of the other inmates and was, therefore, an interesting part to do. If you can lead a life of luxury in prison, Grouty did that. He even had a budgie, which he ended up eating!'

PETER VAUGHAN (Grouty, a prisoner)

'I liked Grouty, he was a great character who came alive in this episode. There's always a Mr Big in prison and we thought it would be interesting to see Fletcher's relationship with him. Peter Vaughan gave this kind of curl on the character and his voice and delivery so we used him again because he'd done a great job.'

IAN LA FRENAIS

GROUTY: That's right. I came back handcuffed to Scotcher of the Yard on Alitalia. I paid the extra and moved us both up into first class. Bit of a perk for him, he's never been south of Worthing before. Bought the Chianti for me, duty free, and got him a bottle of Sambuca.

....

JACKDAW: *(Holding up a packet of bird seed)* Should I feed Seymour, Harry?

GROUTY: Yeah, go on.

FLETCHER: Seymour? Oh, your feathered friend. Very nice.

GROUTY: He's company of an evening. When I was in Parkhurst I had a pigeon.

FLETCHER: Oh, like the Birdman of Alcatraz.

GROUTY: Not really, no.

FLETCHER: No, not really, I suppose. Took a bit more room, though, didn't he? A pigeon.

Memories ...

'Grouty almost ran Slade Prison, as far as the prisoners were concerned. He was a wonderful character and one of our favourites. He was important because he showed that a threat existed for the prisoners, from within their ranks as well as from the screws.

'Peter Vaughan was a superb actor and immediately gobbled up the character of Grouty with enormous glee. My favourite line was when he was talking about having had a pigeon in his previous prison and told Fletcher that he ate it. That made us laugh a great deal; it said a lot about Grouty. Fletcher's reaction was what made you realise that there is a pecking order anywhere, including prison; you have to worry about people both ahead of you and behind you.'

DICK CLEMENT

GROUTY: Just a bit, yeah. On the other hand how else could I keep in touch with the bookmakers?

FLETCHER: Oh I see – yeah.

GROUTY: Brought me in a few bob.

FLETCHER: Yeah, must have done. What did you do with it when you had to leave?

GROUTY: I ate it.

'When a judge sentences you to five years, you don't expect him to come in with you.'

'NO WAY OUT'

Fletcher and Godber organise wine-tasting.

FLETCHER: McLaren, Warren ... I have gathered you here as representatives of your respective cell blocks.

WARREN: What's this all about, Fletch?

FLETCHER: A minute, please. As you know, the festive season is almost upon us.

McLAREN: With all the high spirits and jollity which that entails.

FLETCHER: Now come on, Jock, that's the wrong attitude going in, that is. Let me ask you all what is the real meaning of Christmas? Aside from the shepherds and the swaddling an' that. What comes to mind then?

GODBER: Chestnuts roasting on an open fire.

FLETCHER: What? Oh yes, very good.

McLAREN: What about Mackay roasting on an open fire?

FLETCHER: No, that's Guy Fawkes' night.

WARREN: Crackers. Holly.

GODBER: Treetops glistening and children listening …

FLETCHER: That will do, Godber. You can leave out the Perry Como. I'm talking about what the likes of us associate with Christmas – aside from robbing a postman.

TULIP: What?

FLETCHER: Drink.

WARREN: Drink?

FLETCHER: Drink, yes. That's what everyone does at Christmas, gets drunk. Bombed. Plastered. Elephant's trunk. Legless. Brahms and Liszt as the proverbial newt.

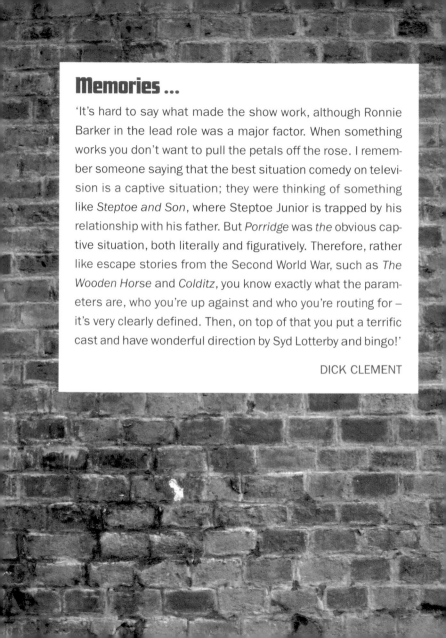

Memories ...

'It's hard to say what made the show work, although Ronnie Barker in the lead role was a major factor. When something works you don't want to pull the petals off the rose. I remember someone saying that the best situation comedy on television is a captive situation; they were thinking of something like *Steptoe and Son*, where Steptoe Junior is trapped by his relationship with his father. But *Porridge* was *the* obvious captive situation, both literally and figuratively. Therefore, rather like escape stories from the Second World War, such as *The Wooden Horse* and *Colditz*, you know exactly what the parameters are, who you're up against and who you're routing for – it's very clearly defined. Then, on top of that you put a terrific cast and have wonderful direction by Syd Lotterby and bingo!'

DICK CLEMENT

GODBER: *(To McLaren)* I've never understood the derivation of that expression myself. Are newts known to be heavy drinkers?

FLETCHER: *(Irritated by the interruption)* Time is somewhat precious. We are running a security risk. Time is somewhat precious.

GODBER: Sorry, Fletch. I was just saying …

FLETCHER: Yuh, well.

TULIP: What are we here for, Fletch?

FLETCHER: Wine-tasting,

The prisoners taste the wine.

GODBER: I'd like to warn you gentlemen, that this should be sipped delicately, like a fine liqueur. It should not be smashed down the throat by the mugful, all right.

Godber passes the cup first to Tulip. He takes a cautious sip and passes it to Warren. He sips and passes it to McLaren who also sips for a moment. Then they react with anguished gasps.

FLETCHER: I thought they'd like it, Len.

WARREN: You ought to have washed the bottle out first.

McLAREN: Fletcher, are you sure this stuff is for human consumption?

FLETCHER: No, I'm not. That's why you three nurks is testing it for me.

···

Fletch and Mackay discuss a tunnel that has been discovered.

MACKAY: It's a harmless question, for future reference. I just want to know how they disposed of the soil?

FLETCHER: They dug another tunnel and put it down there.

Mackay was a no-nonsense prison warder but Fletch still tried pushing the boundaries in pursuit of those 'little victories'.

Memories ...

'This is one of my favourite scenes involving Fulton. It was the end of the Christmas Special when Fletcher is in hospital; Mr Mackay wants to know how they got rid of the soil and brings a bottle of Scotch; Mackay has already had a few because it's Christmas and is slightly tipsy. It's a wonderful performance from Fulton, very subtle and extremely funny.

'I adored Fulton, he was a delight to work with. He was very well-rounded and cultured. He was an artist and keenly interested in everything that was going on. He loved the process of acting and I remember Syd Lotterby saying that Fulton always wanted one more rehearsal, he'd never stop rehearsing. He wanted to keep trying out new things, much more than Ronnie did, who'd say: "Come on Fulton, we've done it, we've got it, let's go." But he was a perfectionist and, in a way, that was dead right for the character. The subtleties in his performance were superb.'

DICK CLEMENT

Memories ...

'Mr Mackay was a great adversarial character and some of the one-on-ones between Ronnie and Fulton were great. Fulton was so professional. He enjoyed himself and had a good time. He liked to know about his character's background and would query anything if it seemed out of character.'

IAN LA FRENAIS

'A STORM IN A TEACUP'

Godber is still in his chef's outfit, washing, when Fletcher enters the cell, carrying his mug of tea and his book.

GODBER: 'Lo, Fletch.

FLETCHER: Oh, they've gone, have they?

GODBER: Who?

FLETCHER: Warren and McLaren – the black and white minstrels.

GODBER: Oh yeah. Hey, I did the lunches on my own today – did you like it?

FLETCHER: Tell me something – what was the name of that pudding?

GODBER: Tapioca.

FLETCHER: Oh, tapioca was it? D'you think you could sneak a dollop back here?

GODBER: P'raps. Like it that much, did you?

FLETCHER: No, but I need something to stick down the sole of my shoe with.

GODBER: I'll ignore that. Can't bait me. Tapioca off a duck's back.

....

Fletch and Grouty discuss missing pills. Grouty demands Fletch's help in finding some replacements.

FLETCHER: Yeah, well that will solve it. Even supposing I can do what you suggest – what am I looking for?

GROUTY: Pills is pills, Fletch. Aspirin, allergy pills, slimming pills.

FLETCHER: Here – those typists are all on the pill. They're all ravers over there.

GROUTY: Now steady on Fletch, there are limits. If you whip those and the MO issues them to some poor bloke with toothache, what then?

FLETCHER: Stop his teeth getting pregnant, won't it.

....

Grouty's life of relative pleasure.

FLETCHER: What a lunch hour. Didn't even have time to finish my cup of tea. And now I've got to get back to work.

'The best things in life aren't free … but the best thing in life is bein' free.'

GROUTY: *(Lying on the bed)* Yes, well, no peace for the wicked.

FLETCHER: Don't you have work to go to, Grouty?

GROUTY: No, I'm on light duties, Fletch. They put me in charge of the swimming pool.

FLETCHER: That's nice, we ain't got one.

GROUTY: I know.

FLETCHER: Oh – clerical error, was it?

GROUTY: Something like that – which is why time hangs so heavy on my hands.

FLETCHER: Oh dear, me. What a shame. Well I'd best be off then. Don't want to interrupt your boredom. Aren't those crystallised fruits over there?

GROUTY: Yes.

FLETCHER: My favourite them.

GROUTY: Really, mine too. Pass them over will you?

'POETIC JUSTICE'

Fletch discovers, much to his chagrin, that he has to share his cell with not just Godber but Judge Rawley, too. To make matters worse, Rawley is none other than the judge who sentenced Fletcher. Godber advises Rawley on prison protocol.

GODBER: Never borrow anything of Fletcher's without express permission.

FLETCHER: I'm not mean, Godber, if that's what you're saying. It's just that I never give anybody anything. What one has one keeps.

GODBER: Oh come on, Fletch. You are mean.

FLETCHER: No, I'm not. Thrifty perhaps. Frugal.

GODBER: He unwraps Bounty Bars under water so I can't hear he's got one.

RAWLEY: I'll be only too willing to share any of the few things they've allowed me.

FLETCHER: Bribery and corruption, he's at it again!

Fletch didn't expect to be sharing a cell with the judge (played by Maurice Denham, left) who put him away.

Memories ...

'Judge Rawley, who was played by Maurice Denham, was born in *On the Rocks*, the American series we wrote. Initially, we used plots from the British series but when they ran out we had to think of new ones; suddenly, we thought about the judge who'd sentenced Fletcher turning up in prison. Having used it in America first, we then translated it for the BBC series. We thought there was a wonderful irony about employing that character. We also had the defrocked dentist in Banyard to represent the occasional posh guy who ends up in prison – after all, they're not all cockneys!'

DICK CLEMENT

RAWLEY: I only meant …

FLETCHER: Just get yourself to bye-byes, Judge Jeffreys.

RAWLEY: Well, let me say that whatever rules you make, I will go along with them.

GODBER: Oh we're very democratic in here – Fletcher decides and we agree.

'ROUGH JUSTICE'

Warren discusses his dyslexia and claims it's the reason for his imprisonment.

WARREN: Dyslexia is word blindness, like. I can't make out words when they're written down. They all get jumbled up in my head.

FLETCHER: Yeah, well there's plenty of room, ain't there?

WARREN: Tragic really. If they'd diagnosed it when I were a lad, I wouldn't be in here now.

FLETCHER: Oh, here we go, the customary alibi – the hard luck story.

Memories ...

'Warren obviously wasn't madly bright and couldn't read or write. He was perfectly amiable but needed help and, therefore, Fletcher was the one he went to because Fletch was not only a survivor but bright, too.

'Ian and I both did National Service so had the experience of living in a hut with a lot of disparate people from different backgrounds; in any environment you always have various characters, such as the assertive bully, the blabbermouth and people like Warren.'

DICK CLEMENT

'Warren was a sweet character and McLaren was great because he was abrasive. Lukewarm was probably a bit broader but still funny. These other characters weren't written as part of a repertory company, we just needed other people and because they were in prison, we'd see them again. So you'd have the recreation set and populate it with your little regular characters.'

IAN LA FRENAIS

WARREN: It's true in my case. I had a real tough break. You see, I couldn't read the sign.

FLETCHER: What sign was this?

WARREN: The one that said, 'Warning – Burglar Alarm'.

....

Rawley returns to the cell, where Warren is talking to Fletch.

RAWLEY: Fletch – oh good evening, Warren.

WARREN: Good evening.

RAWLEY: Fletch, I just bumped into that middle-aged Teddy Boy – what's his name?

GODBER: Harris.

RAWLEY: Yes, very abusive.

FLETCHER: Don't worry about Harris. He's all wind and water. You know what he's in for, don't you? Snatching an old-age pensioner's handbag.

Warren (Sam Kelly) always turned to Fletch, the sage of Slade Prison, for advice.

WARREN: He never!

FLETCHER: At least he tried to. She pinned him down till the cops arrived. She kept hitting him over the head with the hand-bag.

WARREN: And that subdued him?

FLETCHER: Not half – it had a brick in it. She was just on her way to do a smash and grab.

WARREN: Oh blimey.

RAWLEY: Well, he was most abusive.

FLETCHER: Take no notice of Harris.

RAWLEY: But he threatened me.

GODBER: Don't you worry, your Honour. If anyone comes on strong, you know we'll always back you up.

FLETCHER: Yeah, we'll see you all right.

RAWLEY: You already have. And I would like to say how grateful I am to you. You men have every right to despise me. Especially you, Fletch, since I sent you here in the first place. But you have shown me only kindness and compassion. I feel a bond with you men – I know it has been forged in adversity, but I think it will remain with me for the rest of my life.

Memories ...

'*Porridge* worked because it was truthful. Despite the laughs, jokes and hilarious characters there was no doubt that these men were in prison. Acting is about being truthful, nothing else, and we were blessed with two writers who knew that and who could write in no other way.

'Syd Lotterby had used me previously in an episode of *The Liver Birds* and in a one-off sitcom playing, of all things, Cilla Black's boyfriend. To have crossed his mind when casting *Porridge* has helped my career to take off in all directions, both in TV and theatre. Innumerable sitcoms later I give thanks to Syd.

'I remember the hilarious weekly read-throughs, the rehearsals with Ronnie putting in his little looks, double-takes and the odd extra line and Fulton fussing around on his way towards that marvellous performance. I watched relentlessly, instinctively knowing that I was learning all the time.'

SAM KELLY (Warren, a prisoner)

FLETCHER: 'Ere leave it off, Judge. Go on like this, you're going to make us forget our scruples and start liking you.

RAWLEY: No, I meant it. Who'd have thought a few months ago that I could so much as talk to you? Now I find that I respect – more than that – I trust you.

GODBER: You mean that?

RAWLEY: Most sincerely.

He turns to pick up the towel. His expression changes.

RAWLEY: Just a moment. Which one of you stole my watch?

'PARDON ME'

Barrowclough's indecision is the topic of conversation.

FLETCHER: … you know how middle of the road he is on every flaming issue. If you ask for a 'yes' or 'no', he says, 'it depends what you mean by "yes" or "no".'

....

Some of the prisoners are playing Scrabble.

GODBER: Rilk?

FLETCHER: Yes, Rilk.

GODBER: No such bird.

FLETCHER: That is where you are wrong. See, Godber, you're not as smart as you thought you was.

GODBER: What's a flaming Rilk, then?

FLETCHER: The Rilk is a migratory bird from the Baltic shores of North Finland. Its most distinguishable feature is that it flies backwards to keep the snow out of its eyes ... ask me another, Magnus?

Ronnie Barker invested much of his own personality into Fletch while developing the character.

Memories ...

'There was a lot of me in Fletcher – not that I broke into post offices! There was plenty of my father in Fletch, too. Although the character was a Cockney and I was born in Oxford, he was working class and I could relate to him. He was easy to play and I didn't have to think too much about it. Fletcher was obviously a wide-boy, out for everything he could get. Whatever he did was for his own benefit: you think he's helping someone out but he's working it to his own advantage. But Fletch was likeable. You must always have charm in a character; even If you're playing an old tramp you need a bit of charm.'

THE LATE RONNIE BARKER

Blanco is being released.

BLANCO: I'm not very good, you know, at expressing gratitude. But I know what you done … and I'll not forget it.

FLETCHER: You're going out now – all that matters.

GODBER: Got a lot of living to make up for. Don't waste your time nattering with the likes of us.

BLANCO: I don't want much from life.

FLETCHER: I know, but it's good to know that justice has been done – albeit a bit late. This pardon's for your family name, for your children and your grandchildren. That's why we done it. So's you can walk out of here and look any man in the face without shame or guilt. Life's taken a lot from you, me old mate, but all you need back from it is your pride, right?

BLANCO: Right, Fletch.

GODBER: Tarra, Blanco. Keep your nose clean.

BLANCO: So long – same to you, son.

Blanco (David Jason) eventually received a pardon but he wasn't entirely innocent.

FLETCHER: Oh and one more thing, of course.

BLANCO: What?

FLETCHER: You sue the Government for every penny they've got.

BLANCO: Too bloody true, I will.

LUKEWARM: Ta, ta Blanco – I'll miss you.

BLANCO: Thanks for looking after me. I'll try and get that scented notepaper that you want.

Did you know?

Ronnie Barker rated *Porridge* as 'probably the best and most important' show he did, although he believed that for pure fun, *Open All Hours* topped the list.

Memories ...

'When I saw Syd Lotterby about playing the character Lukewarm, I was asked whether I minded playing a homosexual, or an iron hoof, as they said. I didn't mind. I didn't want to make him outrageous so I developed this business that he was always knitting something for his friend, Trevor, who came into "Men Without Women". I didn't receive any complaints from people about how I played Lukewarm. It was still unusual for a gay character to appear in a sitcom, although I'd done it before, playing an outrageous queen in an episode of *Doctor At Sea* and received lots of complaints about that.'

CHRISTOPHER BIGGINS (Lukewarm, a prisoner)

FLETCHER: Here listen – we knows you didn't do in your old lady, which means some other bloke did. And you paid the penance. But don't you go out there harbouring thoughts of revenge.

BLANCO: I know him what did it. It were the wife's lover. But don't you worry, I shan't waste my time looking for him – he's dead.

FLETCHER: Oh that's all right then.

BLANCO: That I do know. It were me that killed him. Cheerio.

'A TEST OF CHARACTER'

Fletcher and Mackay discuss education and backgrounds.

FLETCHER: Yeah, well I never finished school, did I? Never got as far as exams. What was it called – School Certificate in them days.

MACKAY: I can imagine.

FLETCHER: Always playing truant.

MACKAY: Oh yes.

FLETCHER: Well it was the war. We was always on the bomb sites, collecting shrapnel and that. Learning about sex in the air-raid shelters during their off-peak hours. So eventually they sent me to a special school with other kids who were always playing truant. But we never learned nothing.

MACKAY: And why not?

FLETCHER: No one ever turned up for school.

Despite little formal education, Fletch was worldly-wise.

MACKAY: See me, I had to leave school at fourteen. Help bring a living wage into the house. Hard times in those days in the Lanarkshire coalfields. My father was an unemployed miner but there were still eight children to provide for.

FLETCHER: Eight kids, eh? He wasn't unemployed the whole of the time then?

MACKAY: Did I hear you correctly, Fletcher?

FLETCHER: No you didn't, sir.

MACKAY: Let me tell you something, not one of our family neglected education. Not one. Even under the most difficult circumstances like Godber here. I've had to pass exams, you know. *(Picking a book up) The Aspects of the Reformation.* What's the subject you're studying, Godber?

GODBER: History, O-level, like. Already got one O-level before I come inside. Geography.

MACKAY: That's the spirit, laddie. You stick in. And I'm telling you, Fletcher, no I'm ordering you – you do nothing to hinder this lad's concentration, otherwise get out.

Memories ...

'Fulton had plenty of charisma and I thought he played the part impeccably. He was a great actor but occasionally would say: "I can't play this scene, Ronnie." About three-quarters of the rehearsal time was devoted to him, which initially I didn't mind. But eventually I had to say things like: "In this episode I've got twenty-five minutes, you've got five, so can I do a bit of rehearsing as well?" But he was immensely likeable, a charming man, while in character he was the person you loved to hate.'

THE LATE RONNIE BARKER

FLETCHER: I just come in from work – I'm entitled …

MACKAY: You're entitled to nothing in here except to obey the sound of my voice. When's the exam, son?

GODBER: Two days' time.

MACKAY: Right, so make yourself scarce, Fletcher. Is that clear!

He exits.

FLETCHER: *(Calling after him)* All right, all right, I'll go out for the evening! Give us the keys, I'll let meself in. So, can't stay in me own flowery dell in case it upsets his nibs' concentration here.

....

Fletch and Warren's plan to help Godber pass his exam backfires.

WARREN: We're only going to make sure you passes it, aren't we?

GODBER: How?

FLETCHER: By going over the questions with you so you can prepare the appropriate answers.

GODBER: In that case, it would be useful to have the appropriate questions.

FLETCHER: You've got 'em.

From inside his jacket he takes an envelope and throws it in front of Godber.

GODBER: *(Picks it up curiously)* What's this?

FLETCHER: Tomorrow's exam paper. Now shift yourself 'cos we gotta get it back where it come from.

GODBER: The exam paper?

WARREN: Yeah, we did it, didn't we?

Godber hurls the envelope down as if he was scalded.

GODBER: No!

FLETCHER: What do you mean – no?

GODBER: I mean NO. I don't want to cheat. I want to pass this exam honestly!

FLETCHER: Well, of course you do. But honesty is only something you can afford once you made it. And passing this exam is going to help you make it.

Warren (left) and Fletch's attempts to help Godber backfired.

GODBER: Don't you understand? I've cheated all me life. For the first time in my life I want to do something straight.

FLETCHER: Look – once you've passed this exam, no one's going to know how you passed it.

GODBER: I will. Look, if I fail, I fail. But I'm not going to pass through cheating.

FLETCHER: Len, Len. No, no, listen, will you? Lennie, my son, cheating isn't a crime.

Godber looks at him as if to say, 'What are you talking about?'

FLETCHER: 'Course it isn't. Cheating is – getting away with it. World of difference. I mean, everyone cheats.

Did you know?

Although origins of the phrase 'porridge' are unknown, it's believed to date back to the 1830s and is perhaps influenced by stodgy prison food.

WARREN: Listen, Len, you know when you play draughts with Fletch and he says he thinks one fell on the floor and could you pick it up, so you bend down only when you straighten up you find the board's rearranged – that's all cheating is.

FLETCHER: That's right.

WARREN: Oh, so you admit it?

FLETCHER: Name of the game, isn't it? Getting away with it. It's not what you do in life – it's what you get caught doing.

WARREN: And if you don't get caught …

FLETCHER: You're away, ain'tcha? Home and dry.

'FINAL STRETCH'

Godber receives his parole.

GODBER: I owe a lot to you, Fletch. I'd've never made the distance without you.

FLETCHER: Look, don't make me out to be no hero.

GODBER: I wasn't. Father figure maybe.

FLETCHER: I ain't been no great shakes as a dad. Fact, I ain't been no great shakes at anything.

GODBER: You have to me. And I won't let you down, Fletch. I ain't coming back.

FLETCHER: Oh we all say that. But you'd better mean it,

Godber. You've got your life before you. Out of the last twenty years I've spent eleven of 'em doing porridge. That ain't life, that's marking time. I'm not moaning. What's done's done. But it's a terrible waste.

GODBER: I won't be back, given the breaks.

FLETCHER: Make the breaks. No alibis, no ifs and buts. You can make it. You're not stupid, and you're not evil. You're a good lad. Well, nuff said. Hope you're leaving me your snout.

GODBER: Only right.

He gives Fletcher the tobacco from his box.

FLETCHER: Chocolate?

GODBER: Fruit and nut.

He hands Fletcher the chocolate.

Overleaf: Godber owed much to the altruistic Fletcher.

Fletcher prepares for a new cellmate.

MACKAY: Fletcher?

FLETCHER: Good afternoon, sir.

MACKAY: Good afternoon, sir?

FLETCHER: Your title, in' it, sir?

MACKAY: True. I did not expect to hear it so readily from your lips.

'When you chooses your living breaking the law, it pays to know the laws you're breaking.'

FLETCHER: Why make waves, eh? Only ten months to do if I keep my nose clean.

MACKAY: Throwing in the towel, are we Fletcher?

FLETCHER: I just want to go home.

MACKAY: I've noticed a certain change in your attitude since laddo's release. Our customary ill-feeling seems to be missing. You seem to have lost a lot of that brash Cockney lairyness. Or are you just acknowledging that the system always wins.

FLETCHER: Nobody wins, Mr Mackay. That's what's so tragic.

MACKAY: Normally I would have hesitated about putting a sprog in here, Fletcher.

FLETCHER: Oh yes. Got some company coming in, have I?

MACKAY: In the past you have not been the healthiest of influences on first-time offenders. But now I don't think I have too much to fear. Got a young lad called Nicholson moving in.

FLETCHER: Not a Scot, is he? I mean, we do draw the line somewhere.

MACKAY: No, he's from Sunderland.

FLETCHER: Dangerously near.

Memories ...

'You can't underestimate the contribution of all four lead characters. The chemistry between them was great. Brian Wilde's role was the most difficult, in many ways, and he made it work beautifully. He kept getting overlooked in terms of dialogue at times but was a tremendous character, nonetheless.'

IAN LA FRENAIS

MACKAY: He's a tearaway. Lashes out. Doesn't think. I have a feeling that the new quiescent Fletcher might be just what he needs.

FLETCHER: Whatever you think, Mr Mackay.

MACKAY: So you'll keep an eye on him?

FLETCHER: Be difficult to ignore him in a room this size.

MACKAY: No, but perhaps you'll show him the ropes, show him what you've learnt.

FLETCHER: What have I learnt, Mr Mackay?

MACKAY: That there's no point to bucking the system.

FLETCHER: Oh yes. Glad to, Mr Mackay. Sir. I'll watch out for him. I shall simply tell him three things. Bide your time *(puts up one finger)*, keep your nose clean *(two fingers)* and don't let the bastards grind you down *(Fletcher puts up the third finger)*.

TEST YOUR KNOWLEDGE

Do you know your Fletchers from your Godbers, your Mackays from your Barrowcloughs? Why not test yourself with our *Porridge* quiz …

1. Slade Prison was set in which region of England?

2. What was the name of Fletcher's wife?

3. Who played Fletch's son, Raymond, in the sequel, *Going Straight*?

4. When Godber arrived at Slade Prison, he had a fiancée – what was her name?

5. What's the name of the weak-kneed prison governor?

6. Which other lag arrives at Slade Prison the same time as Fletcher and Godber?

7. In which episode does Godber take up boxing?

8. *Porridge* was adapted for the American market – what was the title?

9. Do we witness Fletcher's release in the closing episode, 'Final Stretch'?

10. Where do the writers, Dick Clement and Ian La Frenais, live nowadays?

Answers

1) Cumberland; 2) Isobel; 3) Nicholas Lyndhurst;
4) Denise; 5) Mr Venables; 6) Cyril Heslop;
7) 'The Harder They Fall'; 8) On the Rocks; 9) No;
10) California